CHINESE COOKBOOK

Restaurant Favorites and Authentic Chinese Recipes

(Quick and Easy Dishes to Prepare at Home and a Simple)

Tracy Rose

Published by Sharon Lohan

© Tracy Rose

All Rights Reserved

Chinese Cookbook: Restaurant Favorites and Authentic Chinese Recipes (Quick and Easy Dishes to Prepare at Home and a Simple)

ISBN 978-1-990334-29-0

All rights reserved. No part of this guide may be reproduced in any form without permission in writing from the publisher except in the case of brief quotations embodied in critical articles or reviews.

Legal & Disclaimer

The information contained in this book is not designed to replace or take the place of any form of medicine or professional medical advice. The information in this book has been provided for educational and entertainment purposes only.

The information contained in this book has been compiled from sources deemed reliable, and it is accurate to the best of the Author's knowledge; however, the Author cannot guarantee its accuracy and validity and cannot be held liable for any errors or omissions. Changes are periodically made to this book. You must consult your doctor or get professional medical advice before using any of the suggested remedies, techniques, or information in this book.

Table of contents

Part 1 1

Introduction 2

Chapter One: Basic techniques, appliances and ingredients in Chinese Cooking 3

Chapter Two: Appetizers and Soups 8

Mushroom and chicken soup 9

Chicken with Sweetcorn Soup 11

Hot and sour Szechuan chicken soup 13

Egg Drop Soup 16

Steamed Mushroom and Pork Dumplings 18

Schezuan Cauliflower 21

Chinese Bhel 24

Chinese Style Fried Capsicum 26

Crackling Spinach 28

Dragon Rolls 30

Chapter Three: Main Dishes with Seafood and Meat . 34

Orange Chicken 35

Chicken - Sweet and Sour 39

Chicken Chow Mein 41

Beef Chili with oyster and broccoli sauce 43

Peach Crispy Duck 46

- Sichuan spicy prawns 49
- Sea bass with chili, ginger and spring onions 51
- Crispy pork Chinese-style 53
- Hoisin wraps 55
- Prawn and chorizo fried rice 57
- Chapter Four: Vegetarian Dishes 59
- Egg Fried Rice... 60
- Spicy but sweet tofu 62
- Garlic aubergines 64
- Stir fry veggie noodles... 66
- Spicy Chinese tofu... 69
- Tofu with green vegetables and noodles 72
- Chinese-style long beans... 75
- Chinese cabbage 77
- Sweet potato purple cakes... 79
- Noodle-style pancakes with asparagus 81
- Conclusion 83
- Part 2 85
- Introduction... 86
- Appetizers Recipes 87
- Garlic Snow Peas... 87
- Sweet and Sour Sauce... 89
- Spiced Pecans 92

Prawn Balls	94
Crab Rangoon Dip	96
Shrimp Toast	99
Chinese Spicy Beef Lettuce Wraps	101
Chinese Wontons	103
Chinese Tea Leaf Eggs	106
Spiced Grapes	109
Main dishes	111
Chinese Spareribs	111
Spicy Chinese Barbeque Riblets	114
Chinese Mabo Tofu	116
Chinese Steamed Fish	119
Chinese Pearl Meatballs	121
Chinese Pickled Cucumbers	124
Chinese Braised Zucchini	126
Chinese Buffet Green Beans	128
China Moon Salmon	130
Chinese Broccoli	132
Moo Shu Vegetables	134
Vegetable Lo Mein	136
Chinese Almond Chicken	139
Chinese Roasted Chicken	142
Chinese Stir Fry Vegetables	145

Chinese Peppered Green Beans 147
Chinese-Style Vermicelli 149
Chinese Chicken Fried Rice 151
Easy Fried Spinach 153
Hot and Sour Chinese Eggplant 155
Chicken and Chinese Noodles Casserole 157
Chinese Garlic Chicken 160
Chinese Pepper Round Steak 162
Ground Beef Chinese Casserole 164
Chinese Curry Chicken 167
Soup recipes 170
Chinese Sizzling Rice Soup 170
Chinese Chicken Soup 173
Chinese Glass Noodle Soup 175
Chinese Shrimp and Tofu Soup 177
Chinese Corn Soup 179
Chinese Egg Soup 182
Quick Veggie Soup 183
Dessert recipes 185
Chinese Restaurant Almond Cookies 185
Chinese Christmas Cookies 187

Part 1

Introduction

There is nothing quite like ordering a Chinese takeaway and having that delicious food delivered to your door and opening up those wonderful containers, with that great smell wafting through.

There is something about the anticipation and the sheer indulgence of having someone else cook for you. There is also an element of the exotic about Chinese food – the specific flavors, the smells and the tastes – which make it easy to believe that it's difficult to create.

But the key element which makes Chinese dishes so special is the sheer simplicity of most of them. The techniques outlined in this book will give you the know-how to make these dishes for yourself, with very little difficulty.

From the classic stir fry to dumplings, wontons and hot and spicy soups, all of your favorites from the Chinese menu can now be created with little effort, in the comfort of your own kitchen.

The secret here is that most of the techniques used to create the dishes that we love are surprisingly quick and easy to do. Nothing could be simpler than stir frying fresh ingredients and spices together in a hot work to create an amazing dish.

Chapter One: Basic techniques, appliances and ingredients in Chinese Cooking

Chinese cookery is famous throughout the globe for its distinctive flavors and style, and its healthy properties. There is an emphasis on simple techniques, easy recipes and the use of fresh ingredients which are prepared with little fuss and balanced beautifully.

In this chapter, you will learn:

- The key cooking methods to create Chinese dishes
- The equipment you will need in your kitchen
- How to stock your pantry for Chinese food?

There are a number of key cooking methods which you need to be aware of if you are going to try to create authentic Chinese dishes at home, which will compete with your local take away in terms of flavor, but also provide you with some healthy options.

Stir-Frying

Stir-frying is one of the most traditional and classic methods of Chinese cooking as it is quick, easy and creates dishes full of flavor. Generally, dishes which are stir fried would involve meat, seafood, tofu or veggies. Stir frying is normally carried out in a wok which needs to be heated up to a high heat level before any ingredients are added to the pan.

Deep-Frying

Deep-frying is used in Chinese cookery when you want to create crispy and textured food. This technique is generally used to fry meat or vegetables. It is normally carried out in a deep pan or fryer.

Steaming

Steaming is a common and healthy Chinese cooking technique. Steaming ingredients can make any dish taste fresher. It also helps to retain the nutrients within the food. In China, food is steamed using bamboo steamers, which can be stacked on top of each other.

Red Stewing or Red-Cooking

Red stewing is a completely unique technique for Chinese cooking and is used for cooking tough meat. The food is cooked very slowly over a low heat and it can take several hours before the meat is at the right tenderness.

Boiling

Boiling is one of the most simple Chinese techniques, it is quicker than others and preserves the texture and integrity of the ingredients. Boiled ingredients are generally served immediately after cooking.

Roasting

The meat is prepared and then roasted in a very hot oven until the skin is crispy.

Braising

Braising involves putting all of the ingredients into a pan and boiling it to start with, then simmering at a lower temperature for an hour or more afterward.

If you are to carry out the outlined Chinese techniques, there are a few specific cooking utensils and appliances which you will need to make Chinese dishes successfully at home.

Chinese Cleaver – a specialist cleaver designed to chop through bone, which is used for meat dishes, as well as crushing garlic and ginger. They are normally made out of steel.

Wok – this is one of the most common Chinese cooking utensils and can be found in most kitchens. It is a large pan and used for stir frying largely but can also be used to carry out most of the cooking techniques outlined here.

Wok Shovel – this is a tool which is designed for stir-frying and scooping food while cooking in woks.

Chopsticks - the cooking variety can be used to pick food out of pans, such as noodles or chunks of meat. The eating variety can also be used in the kitchen for mixing ingredients together.

Rice Cooker – this is an electric cooker used for boiling or steaming rice and is more efficient than cooking on the hob. They can also be used for other dishes such as stewing meat and steaming eggs.

Steaming Baskets – these are used commonly in China and can be used to steam all sorts of food including fish, meat, pancakes and dumplings. They can be stacked on top of each other allowing various dishes to be cooked at the same time.

Now that you have the tools, what ingredients do you need to stock your cupboard with to get started? There are a number of staple ingredients that are needed for all Chinese cooking so stock up on these and you are ready to get going.

- Oyster sauce
- Rice
- Rice vinegar
- Rice wine
- Dried Chinese mushrooms
- Soy sauce

- Toasted sesame oil
- Chili sauce
- Dark soy sauce
- Fermented black beans
- Fresh ginger
- Hoisin sauce

Chapter Two: Appetizers and Soups

From hot and sour soups, to crispy rolls and prawn balls, we all have our favorite Chinese starter. In this chapter you will find a variety of Chinese appetizers and soups which you can make in your kitchen.

In this chapter, you will learn:

- Hot and Sour Soups

- Perfect Dumplings

- Surprising dishes with spinach

Mushroom and chicken soup

Serves: two
Prep time: 1hr 30 min
Cook time: 10 min
Calories: 137

Ingredients

For the stock

- Bones from a chicken

- Three peppercorns

- Two bay leaves

- Two onions, skin still on, cut in half

- Water

- Pepper

For the soup

- A cooked and shredded chicken breast

- Two sliced big mushrooms

- Two sliced spring onions

Directions:

- Add the bones to a saucepan to start making the stock

- Put the onions, pepper, bay leaves, peppercorns and enough water into the pot to cover it all

- Boil the mixture and then leave to simmer for around two hours

- You can make the stock in advance and keep it in the fridge

- Put the stock through a fine sieve

- When you are about to make the soup, warm the stock up in a pan, by bringing to boil and then leaving to simmer

- Put the mushrooms and the shredded chicken into the pan and warm it through for about five minutes

Tip: Serve the soup in bowls, garnished with the onions

Chicken with Sweetcorn Soup

Serves: four
Prep time: 10 min
Cook time: 15 min
Calories: 66

Ingredients

- 800 milliliters of chicken stock
- 420 grams of cream style tinned corn
- 75 grams of cooked and shredded chicken
- A quarter of a teaspoon of ground white pepper
- salt
- Two tablespoons of cornflour
- 125 milliliters of water
- A tablespoon of sesame oil
- An egg white
- Spring onions – for the garnish

Directions:

- Mix together the stock, the chicken and the corn in a pan

- Bring the mixture to the boil before lowering the heat and then seasoning

- Bring it back up to boil

- Mix together the water and cornflour

- Add the cornflour mixture to the soup while it is still boiling and mix well

- Add in several drops of sesame oil

- Turn down the heat and mix the egg white gradually into the soup, ensuring it is thoroughly broken down

Tip: Serve hot with the garnish.

Hot and sour Szechuan chicken soup

Serves: Four
Prep time: 10 minutes
Cook time: 20 minutes
Calories: 267

Ingredients

- 750 milliliters of chicken stock
- 100 milliliters of water
- 200 grams of freshly sliced mushrooms
- 50 grams of bamboo shoots
- Three slices of ginger
- Two crushed garlic cloves
- A tablespoon of soy sauce
- A quarter of a teaspoon of dried chilies
- 500 grams of chicken breast fillets, cut into strips. Skinless and boneless
- A tablespoon of sesame oil
- Two chopped spring onions
- A handful of fresh coriander
- Three tablespoons of white wine vinegar

- Two tablespoons of cornflour

- A beaten egg

Directions:

- Put the chicken stock, bamboo shoots, ginger, water, mushrooms, soy sauce, garlic and crushed chilies into a saucepan

- Bring the pan to the boil, then leave to simmer, covered

- Put the chicken strips in a bowl with the sesame oil and toss to coat

- Take another bowl and mix the vinegar with the cornflour, leave it to one side

- Turn the heat up under the pan and bring to a boil

- Put the chicken into the pan

- Return the pan to the boil, and slowly add the egg into the mixture, stirring to create strands of egg white

- Add the cornflour and vinegar

- Keep the mixture simmering over a medium level heat, and stir every now and then, until the chicken is cooked and the stock has thickened – should take around three minutes

Tip: Serve the dish with a spring onion and coriander garnish

Egg Drop Soup

Serves: Five
Prep time:10 minutes
Cook time:10 minutes
Calories: 267

Ingredients

- Chicken broth – 4/5 cups
- 2 tbsp chives – chopped
- 1/6 tbsp ground ginger
- 2 tbsp cornstarch
- 5 eggs
- 1 egg yolk
- Salt to taste

Directions:

- Pour ½ cup of your chicken broth into a saucepan. Set aside the rest for later.
- Add salt, ginger, chives to the pan and stir, bringing to a boil.
- In a bowl mix together the rest of your broth and cornstarch.

- In another bowl combine the eggs and egg yolk with a fork.

- Drizzle the egg mixture slowly into the boiling broth. It should take seconds for the eggs to cook.

- Add the cornstarch mixture once the eggs are cooked and stir gradually until you are satisfied with the soup consistency.

Steamed Mushroom and Pork Dumplings

Cook time: 25 minutes
Prep time: 12-14
Serves: 4
Calories: 330

Ingredients

The Filling

- 115 grams of pork - ground
- Three chopped shiitake mushrooms
- One chopped large spring onion – only the green part
- A tablespoon of grated ginger
- A tablespoon of light soy sauce
- A tablespoon of dry sherry or rice wine
- A teaspoon of toasted sesame oil
- Salt
- Black pepper
- Two teaspoons of cornflour

The Dumplings

- Ten square wonton wrappers

- Fifteen goji berries

- Vegetable oil

The Dipping Sauce

- A tablespoon of hot chili sauce

- A tablespoon of light soy sauce

Directions:

- Put all of the filling ingredients into a large bowl and mix

- Lay out a wonton wrapper. Put a large teaspoon of the filling into the center of the wrapper

- Pull up all of the sides of the wrapper and shape them around the filling, creating a ball, but leave the center open

- Put your finger into some water and gently brush it across the top of the wrapper all the way round

- Then fold the rest of the wrapper down and then pinch it firmly around the filling so it can't open and split from the filling once cooked

- Put a berry on top of each dumpling

- Prepare the bamboo steamer

- Put the dumplings into the steamer, put the lid on and put it over a pan of boiling water

- Steam them until cooked – should be about 7-8 minutes

- Mix both the chili sauce and soy sauce in a bowl. Serve the mixture with the dumplings

Tip: You can swap out goji berries for other savory vegetables

Schezuan Cauliflower

Prep time: 15 minutes
Cook time: 15 minutes
Serves: 3
Calories: 154

Ingredients

- Two cups of cauliflower florets
- Oil for frying
- Two tablespoons of oil
- A tablespoon of garlic, chopped
- Half a teaspoon of ginger, chopped
- Half a teaspoon of green chilies, chopped
- A quarter of a cup of spring onions, chopped
- Five tablespoons of <u>schezuan sauce</u>
- A tablespoon of tomato ketchup
- One pinch of sugar
- Salt

Batter mix

- Half a cup of plain flour

- A quarter of a cup of cornflour
- One teaspoon of oil
- Salt
- Half a cup of water

Garnish

- Two tablespoons of chopped spring onion – green only

Directions:

- Heat up the oil in a fryer.
- Coat the cauliflower florets in the batter mixture and deep fry. Once golden brown, remove from the oil and drain on paper.
- Heat some more oil in a frying pan. Put in the green chilies, ginger and garlic and cook on a high heat for just a couple of seconds
- Put the spring onions into the pan and cook on a high heat for a minute
- Put the ketchup, salt, sugar and schezuan sauce into the pan. Mix all together and cook on a high heat for half a minute
- Toss the cooked cauliflower lightly into the sauce and cook on a high heat for a couple of minutes

- Serve immediately with the garnish

Tip: The cauliflower is likely to become soggy the longer you leave it so best to serve this dish immediately

Chinese Bhel

Prep time: 15 mins
Cook time: 2 mins
Makes 2 servings
Calories: 455

Ingredients

- Three cups of fried noodles
- One tablespoon of oil
- Two teaspoons of garlic, chopped
- One-quarter of a cup of chopped spring onion
- Half a cup of sliced capsicum
- Half a cup of chopped carrot
- Half a cup of shredded cabbage
- Half a cup of schezuan sauce
- A quarter of a cup tomato ketchup
- Salt

Garnish

- Two tablespoons of spring onions, chopped

Directions:

- Put the oil in a pan and cook the garlic on a high heat for a few seconds

- Put the carrots, cabbage, capsicum and spring onions and on a high heat for half a minute

- Put the salt, ketchup and the schezuan sauce together, mix, cook high for several seconds

- Take the food off the heat and put into a bowl

- Put the noodles into the bowl and mix together

Tip: Serve immediately with the garnish

Chinese Style Fried Capsicum

Prep time: 10 mins
Cook time: 15 mins
Makes 2 servings
Calories: 239

Ingredients

The Sauce

- Five tablespoons of chopped coriander
- A tablespoon of green chilies, chopped
- Two tablespoons of sugar
- Two tablespoons of garlic, chopped
- One tablespoon of lemon juice
- Salt
- Two teaspoons of vinegar

For The Fried Capsicum

- Half a cup of capsicum wedges
- Half a cup of plain flour
- A quarter of a cup of cornflour
- Salt

- A teaspoon of chili powder
- Half a teaspoon of mustard powder
- Oil to deep fry

Directions:

The garlic sauce

- Put all the ingredients into a bowl and mix together
- Leave it to one side to settle for half an hour

The fried capsicum

- Put all of the ingredients into a bowl and mix together with half a cup of water
- Heat the oil in a pan. Dip the capsicum into batter and deep fry until golden brown
- Drain them on paper
- Serve straight away with the sauce

Tip: Replace capsicum with 1 cup of water thickly sliced baby corn and proceed as per the recipe.

Crackling Spinach

Prep time: 10 minutes
Cook time: 15 minutes
Makes 4 servings
Calories: 209

Ingredients

- Four cups of shredded spinach
- Oil to deep fry
- A teaspoon of oil
- Four teaspoons of chopped garlic
- Four teaspoons of sesame seeds
- One tablespoon of sugar
- Salt

Directions:

- Heat up the oil to deep fry, in a large pan, and put some of the spinach in the strainer
- Fry the spinach in the strainer for 2-3 minutes
- Take the spinach out of the strainer, and drain it on paper

- Fry the rest of the spinach gradually and keep to one side

- Warm up the oil in a pan and put the sesame seeds and garlic into the pan

- Once the seeds start to crackle, put the spinach in, along with the sugar and salt

- Serve immediately

Tip: Shred the spinach, wash it with water and drain well. Spread it on a muslin cloth and let it dry.

Dragon Rolls

Prep time: 20 minutes
Cook time: 20 minutes
Makes: 12 dragon rolls
Calories: 100 per roll

Ingredients

The Wonton Wrappers

- Half a cup of plain flour
- A quarter of a teaspoon of salt
- A teaspoon of oil

The Filling

- A quarter of a cup of red cabbage, shredded
- A quarter of a cup of cabbage, shredded
- A quarter of a cup of red capsicum, sliced
- Three-quarters of a cup of bean sprouts
- A quarter of a cup of sliced carrot
- A tablespoon of oil
- Two teaspoons of garlic, chopped
- One pinch of sugar
- Salt

- One tablespoon of schezuan sauce

Other

- One tablespoon of plain flour

- Plain flour for rolling

- Oil to deep fry

To serve
  - Schezuan sauce

Directions:

The wonton wrapper

- Sieve together the plain flour with the salt into a bowl and use two tablespoons of water to knead it all together into a soft dough

- Add the oil into the dough and then knead some more

- Cover the dough with a damp cloth and put it to one side for half an hour

The filling

- Heat the oil in a pan. Put the garlic in the pan and heat it on a medium heat for just a few seconds

- Put all of the rest of the ingredients, apart from the schezuan sauce, into the pan and cook on a high heat for 2 to 3 minutes.

- Then add in the schezuan sauce, combine well together and cook over medium heat for a minute

- Mix together the plain flour with a tablespoon of water, in a bowl. Put it to one side

- Separate the dough into 12 equal sections and then roll each section into a 100-millimetre circle using some plain flour to roll it out

- Put one of the wonton wrappers onto a dry surface, and put a tablespoon of the filling onto the wrapper

- Make some plain flour-water paste and put it on the edge of the wrapper

- Fold over the top side of the wrapper, across the filling and seal it well

- Fold over the right side and left sides of the wrapper across towards the middle

- Roll the top side of the wrapper, making sure the filling is downwards. Seal the end tightly with the flour-water paste

- Repeat until you have made 12 rolls in total

- Warm up the oil in a deep pan and fry a couple of rolls over a medium heat. Wait until they are golden brown and then drain on a paper

- Serve with the sauce

Tip: Make these as hot and spicy as you can stand by adjusting the spice levels

Chapter Three: Main Dishes with Seafood and Meat

In this chapter you will find recipes for some of the classic Chinese dishes that we all love. With rice and noodle dishes, flavorsome duck and chicken dishes and some of the more unusual fish recipes, there is something to suit all taste buds included in this next chapter.

In this chapter, you will learn:

- Seafood Dishes with Classic Chinese Flavors
- Unusual Chicken Dishes with a Chinese Twist
- Stir Fries and Noodle Dishes

Orange Chicken

Serves: Four
Prep time: 40 minutes
Cook time: 40 minutes
Extra time: 2hrs
Calories: 380

Ingredients

Sauce

- 350 milliliters of water

- 30 milliliters of orange juice

- 60 milliliters of lemon juice

- 80 milliliters of rice vinegar

- 40 milliliters of soy sauce

- A tablespoon of orange zest, grated

- 100 grams of brown soft sugar

- Half a teaspoon of ginger

- Half a teaspoon of garlic

- Two tablespoons of spring onion, chopped

- A quarter of a teaspoon of chili flakes

- Three tablespoons of cornflour
- Two tablespoons of water

Chicken

- Two chicken breasts, cut into small pieces – skin and boneless
- 125 grams of plain flour
- A quarter of a teaspoon of salt
- A quarter of a teaspoon of pepper
- Three tablespoons of olive oil

Directions:

- Take a saucepan and pour in 350 milliliters of water, the rice vinegar, lemon juice, soy sauce and orange juice together and cook over a medium heat
- Add in the brown sugar, garlic, onion, chili flakes, ginger and orange zest and stir in well
- Bring the mixture up to boil. Then remove it from the heat and leave to cool down for 10 to 15 minutes.
- Put all of the chicken pieces into a plastic bag

- Once the saucepan contents have cooled down then pour 250 milliliters of the sauce into the bag with the chicken

- Keep the rest of the sauce aside.

- Seal the bag with the chicken and keep in the fridge for two hours

- Take a second bag and put into it the salt and pepper mixed with the flour

- Put the marinated chicken pieces into the bag containing the flour mix and shake well to ensure the chicken is thoroughly coated

- Warm up the olive oil in a frying pan over a medium flame

- Put the chicken in the pan, and cook on both sides

- Drain the chicken on a plate, then cover with foil

- Clean out the pan, add the sauce and bring to the boil over a medium heat

- Mix the cornflour with two tablespoons of water and stir this into the sauce

- Turn the heat down low, put the chicken in and simmer for five minutes, while stirring

Tip: the longer you marinade the meat the stronger the flavors

Chicken - Sweet and Sour

Serves: Four
Prep time: 10 minutes
Cook time: 10 minutes
Calories: 654

Ingredients

- 500 grams of diced chicken breasts
- Two tablespoons of vegetable oil
- Half a sliced green pepper
- Half a sliced red pepper
- Two sliced carrots
- A garlic clove, crushed
- A tablespoon of cornflour
- Four tablespoons of soy sauce
- A small tin of pineapple pieces, with the juice separated
- One tablespoon of rice vinegar
- One tablespoon of light brown soft sugar
- Half a teaspoon of ground ginger

Directions:

- Heat the oil in a large pan over a medium heat until the chicken is browned

- Put the garlic, carrot, green pepper and red pepper into the pan and stir-fry for two minutes

- Take a small bowl, and mix together the cornflour and soy sauce

- Add the mixture to the frying pan. Add the vinegar, sugar, pineapple and ginger

- Stir all of the ingredients well before bringing to the boil

Tip: Serve with rice to bring out the flavors and create a filling dish

Chicken Chow Mein

Serves: four
Prep time: 25 minutes
Cook time: 15 minutes
Calories: 545

Ingredients

- 250 grams of egg noodles
- Two tablespoons of oil
- One tablespoon of sesame oil
- Two chopped garlic cloves
- Four chicken breasts, cut thinly
- One large red pepper, chopped
- 110 grams of tinned sweetcorn
- Eight trimmed spring onions
- Three tablespoons of light soy sauce

Directions:

- Boil the noodles in a pan until cooked
- Warm up the two oils in a pan, add the garlic and fry for half a minute

- Put the chicken into the pan and stir-fry for five minutes

- Take the chicken out of the pan and set to one side

- Put the pepper into the pan and stir-fry for around four minutes, put in the sweetcorn then stir-fry for another minute

- Put the spring onions in the pan and stir-fry for another minute

- Put the chicken and the noodles into the pan

- Put the soy sauce into the mixture and warm through, mixing well for around two minutes

Tip: Try replacing the chicken for alternative versions to this classic dish

Beef Chili with oyster and broccoli sauce

Prep time: 15 minutes
Cook time: 15 minutes
Calories: 408
Serves: four

Ingredients

- 500 grams of rump steak, sliced
- Two tablespoons of soy sauce
- A large pinch of five spice
- Two tablespoons of rice wine or dry sherry
- One sliced red chili
- Two tablespoons of cornflour
- Three tablespoons of sunflower oil
- Two seeded and chopped peppers
- 150 grams of broccoli, trimmed
- 200 milliliters of chicken stock
- Two tablespoons of oyster sauce
- rice or noodles

Directions:

- Put the sliced beef into a bowl, along with the five spice, the rice wine, soy sauce, chili, cornflour and then season it with the pepper

- Mix it really well so that the beef is completely coated and then leave the meat to marinate for between 10 minutes and a half an hour

- Put two tablespoons of oil into a wok over a high heat

- Start to put the beef into the wok. It needs to be cooked in a single layer, so try cooking it in batches if need be

- Fry the beef on a high heat for around three minutes until it is brown and crisp, and then put it onto a plate

- Once the beef is cooked, wipe the wok out

- Heat up the rest of the oil. Stir fry the broccoli with the peppers for around a minute.

- Pour the stock over the vegetables and then stir in the oyster sauce

- Let everything simmer in for around a minute before adding the beef to the wok. Boil the whole mixture briefly to help the sauce thicken

- Serve with your choice of rice or noodles

Tip: Use a cheaper cut of meat to fully tenderize it with the marinade

Peach Crispy Duck

Prep time: 35 minutes
Cook time: 3 hrs. 5 minutes
Calories: 809
Serves: five

Ingredients

- A duck - 4lb 8oz-5lb 8oz
- A peach
- Two teaspoons of five spice
- Two teaspoons of Sichuan pepper
- Two teaspoons of salt
- Jasmine rice
- Spring onions

For the peaches

- Five halved, destoned peaches
- Two tablespoons of honey
- Two tablespoons of rice wine vinegar
- Three tablespoons of sesame oil
- Two tablespoons of ginger, chopped

- Six tablespoons of hoisin sauce
- Two teaspoons of toasted sesame seeds

Directions

- Heat the oven to either 140C, or 120C for a fan oven, or gas mark 1
- Take a fork and gently prick the duck skin with a fork – not too deep
- Take the whole peach and put it directly into the duck cavity. Tuck any extra fat inside and then tie its legs
- Grind the pepper, five spice and salt together
- Rub the salt mixture over the duck. Put the duck breast-side down in a roasting tin and then into the oven
- Roast the duck in the oven for three hours
- Place the peaches, cut side up, into an oven proof dish
- Mix together the hoisin, vinegar, honey, sesame oil, ginger and three tablespoons of water, in a bowl
- Pour the mixture over the peaches. Sprinkle the sesame seeds over the peaches

- Once cooked, take the duck out of the oven. Drain out any fat

- Turn the oven up higher to 200C or 180C for a fan oven, or gas mark 6. Turn the duck over so the breast is facing up

- Roast the duck for a further half an hour, with the peaches in the tin on the shelf underneath. Cook until the peaches are soft and the duck is crisp

Tip: Serve with the rice and garnish

Sichuan spicy prawns

Prep time: 25 minutes
Cook time: 5 minutes
Calories: 156
Serves: Four

Ingredients

- One and a half tablespoons of groundnut oil
- Two cm piece of ginger, chopped
- Two chopped cloves of garlic
- A chopped spring onion
- 450 grams of prawns

For the sauce

- A tablespoon of tomato purée
- Three teaspoons of chili bean sauce
- Two teaspoons of cider vinegar
- Two teaspoons of golden caster sugar
- Two teaspoons of sesame oil
- A handful of coriander
- One spring onion, sliced

Directions:

- Put the wok on a high heat

- Put the groundnut oil into the pan. Once it is so hot that it smokes, put in the garlic, the ginger and the spring onions

- Stir fry the mixture for around 20 seconds before adding in the prawns

- Keep frying for around a minute.

- Add in all the rest of the sauce ingredients as well as half a teaspoon of salt and half a teaspoon of pepper

- Stir fry for a further three minutes over a high heat

Tip: Serve the dish immediately with the garnish

Sea bass with chili, ginger and spring onions

Prep time: 15 minutes
Cook time: 10 minutes
Calories: 202
Serves: six

Ingredients

- Six fillets of sea bass, scaled but with the skin left on
- Three tablespoons of sunflower oil
- Ginger chopped into matchsticks
- Three sliced garlic cloves
- Three deseeded and chopped red chilies
- Chopped spring onions
- A tablespoon of soy sauce

Directions:

- Sprinkle the fillets with the salt and pepper and slash the skin several times
- Warm up a frying pan with a tablespoon of oil
- Once the pan is hot, fry the fillets skin side down, for around five minutes, until the skin is crisp

- Turn this fish over and then cook for a further 30 seconds to a minute. Transfer the fish to a plate and keep them warm

- You will need to cook the fish in two lots

- Warm up the remaining oil. Fry up the garlic, chilies and ginger for around two minutes

- Remove the mixture from the heat and throw in the spring onions

- Put soy sauce over the fish and then pour the sauce from the pan over the fillets and serve

Tip: Make sure the fish is thoroughly cooked through before transferring to the plates

Crispy pork Chinese-style

Prep time: 10 minutes
Plus at least 2 hours salting
Calories: 696
Serves: four

Ingredients

- 1.3-kilogramme piece of boned pork belly, with the skin on and scored

- Two teaspoons of five spice

For the dipping sauce

- Four tablespoons of soy sauce

- A small piece of grated ginger

- A tablespoon of Thai sweet chili sauce

- A chopped spring onion

Directions:

- Take the pork and rub it with both the five spice mixture and the two teaspoons of salt. Leave it in the fridge for about two hours, but preferably overnight, uncovered

- Put the oven on its highest setting

- Put the pork on a rack over a roasting tray, leaving the skin exposed

- Roast the pork for around 10 minutes, then turn the heat down to around 180C or 160C for a fan oven, or gas mark 4. Leave it to cook for another 1½ hours.

- Check the pork – if the skin is not yet crispy then increase the heat to 220C or 200C for a fan oven, or gas mark 7 and cook it for another half an hour until it's crispy

- Let the pork rest on a plate for 10 minutes

- Now make the sauce by mixing all of the ingredients with two tablespoons of water

- Chop the pork into small sections and serve with the sauce

Tip: Pork belly can either be tied into a joint and roasted, or roasted as a flat piece

Hoisin wraps

Prep time: 5 minutes
Cook time: 5 minutes
Calories: 302
Serves: 2

Ingredients

- 200 grams of turkey or chicken, cooked and in strips
- Four tablespoons of hoisin sauce
- Two flour tortillas
- A quarter of a cucumber, shredded
- Four shredded spring onions
- A handful of watercress

Directions:

- Set the grill to a high heat
- Use half of the hoisin sauce to coat the meat. Spread the meat in an ovenproof dish and grill it
- Warm up the tortillas under the grill as well
- Take the rest of the hoisin sauce and spread it on the tortillas. Then use them to wrap up the meat, along with the onions, cucumber and watercress.

Tip: Serve cut in half while still warm

Prawn and chorizo fried rice

Prep time: 10 minutes
Cook time: 18 minutes
Calories: 404
Serves 2

Ingredients

- 100 grams of either basmati rice or long grain rice
- 85 grams of frozen peas
- A tablespoon of sunflower oil
- A beaten egg
- 50 grams of chopped bacon, chorizo or ham
- A chopped clove of garlic
- Three spring onions, sliced
- Half a chopped, deseeded red pepper
- A pinch of five spice
- A teaspoon of soy sauce
- 100 grams of bean sprouts
- 50 grams of peeled prawns

Directions:

- Boil the rice and the peas and then drain
- Warm up half of the oil in the wok
- Pour the egg into the wok and scramble it
- Put the egg on a plate and leave to one side
- Clean the wok and then heat the rest of the oil up
- Put the garlic, spring onions, meat and pepper into the wok and stir fry
- Put the rice, peas, soy and five spice into the wok and stir-fry for another five minutes
- Add the beansprouts with the prawns and the eggs and heat through

Tip: Make sure the egg is well cooked before taking out of the wok

Chapter Four: Vegetarian Dishes

Some of the best-loved Chinese meals such as vegetable spring rolls and egg fried rice, don't feature any meat or fish at all. With many Chinese vegetables providing fresh flavors and adding crunch to meals, for a healthier option, why not explore some of the vegetarian dishes here. If you are not a vegetarian, you can always substitute the tofu for fish or chicken.

In this chapter, you will learn:

- Rice and Noodle Dishes
- Best Tofu Recipes

Egg Fried Rice

Serves: Four
Prep time: 5 minutes
Cook time: 15 minutes
Calories: 679

Ingredients

- 225 grams of water

- Half a teaspoon of salt

- Two tablespoons of soy sauce

- 75 grams of uncooked rice

- A teaspoon of vegetable oil

- Half a chopped onion

- 100 grams of green beans

- A lightly beaten egg

- One-quarter of a teaspoon of pepper

Directions:

- Take a saucepan and add the salt, soy sauce and water, and bring the mixture to the boil

- Add the rice into the pan and stir. Once cooked, remove it from the heat, cover it and let it stand for five minutes

- Heat the oil up in a wok, over a medium heat and cook the onions and green beans for a few minutes. Add the egg and fry together for a few minutes, making sure to scramble the egg while cooking

- Stir the cooked rice into the mixture as well and season to taste

Tip: The ideal way to take leftover rice and turn it into something delicious

Spicy but sweet tofu

Serves: four
Prep time: 10 minutes
Cook time: 12 minutes
Calories: 323

Ingredients

- Three tablespoons of groundnut oil
- 900 grams of cubed tofu
- A sliced red onion
- A sliced red pepper
- A chopped green chili
- Three cloves of garlic
- Five tablespoons of hot water
- Three tablespoons of white wine vinegar
- Three tablespoons of soy sauce
- A tablespoon of dark brown sugar
- One teaspoon of corn flour
- One teaspoon of chilies

Directions:

- Heat the oil in a wok-style pan over medium heat

- Put the tofu into the oil and fry until brown on all sides

- Add in the chili, garlic, onion and red pepper into the pan and cook with the tofu until tender

- Whisk the chilies, cornflour, vinegar, soy sauce, brown sugar and hot water together in a bowl

- Pour the sauce over the tofu and vegetable mixture, mix well to coat the tofu and then simmer for around five minutes until the sauce gets thicker

Tip: If you like your dishes mild then leave out the chilies or just decrease the amount

Garlic aubergines

Serves: six

Prep time:10 minutes

Cook time: 15 minutes

Calories: 53

Ingredients

- Three tablespoons of rapeseed oil
- Four Chinese aubergines – halve them lengthways, cut into small semi-circles
- 250 milliliters of water
- A tablespoon of crushed chilies
- Three tablespoons of garlic
- Five teaspoons of caster sugar
- A teaspoon of corn flour
- Two tablespoons of light soy sauce
- Two tablespoons of oyster sauce

Directions:

- Heat the oil over a high heat in a frying pan. Cook the aubergine until soft – it will take around four minutes

- Add the garlic, chilies and water into the pan. Cover the mixture and simmer. Leave until all of the water has been soaked up

- Take a bowl and mix together the soy sauce, corn flour, sugar and oyster sauce, until the flour and sugar are both dissolved completely

- Stir the sauce mixture into the pan with the aubergine, coating it completely. Cook through until the sauce is thick

Tip: Chinese aubergines look like purple courgettes but normal aubergines can be used just as easily.

Stir fry veggie noodles

Serves: four

Prep time: 15 minutes

Cook time:10 minutes

Calories: 361

Ingredients

- Two and a half tablespoons of soy sauce
- Three tablespoons of sake
- Two tablespoons of balsamic vinegar
- Two teaspoons of caster sugar
- Three tablespoons of water
- Two teaspoons of corn flour
- A tablespoon of rapeseed oil
- Two tablespoons of toasted sesame oil
- Two sliced garlic cloves
- Six complete dried red chilies, seeded and chopped
- A tablespoon of ginger
- A medium head of pak choi, chopped into strips

- Twenty shiitake mushrooms, stemmed and chopped
- Eight spring onions cut lengthways
- 515 grams of rice noodles
- Two tablespoons of toasted sesame seeds

Directions:
- Whisk together the water, sake, sugar, corn flour, and soy sauce in a small bowl
- Heat the oil in a wok over a high heat level
- Wait until the oil is almost smoking and put the garlic and chilies in
- After around 10 seconds, remove from the heat
- Lower the heat to medium and put the wok back on
- Put the pak choi, ginger, mushrooms and spring onions into the wok and cook on a high heat level for around three minutes
- Put the rice noodles and the soy sauce mixture into the wok as well, cook for a further two minutes until the noodles are soft
- Serve immediately, sprinkled with toasted sesame seeds

Tip: You can use rehydrated dry rice noodles and dry shiitakes if easier and sherry can replace sake.

Spicy Chinese tofu

Serves: two

Prep time: 20 minutes

Cook time:10 minutes

Marinade time:30 minutes

Calories: 307

Ingredients

- 200 grams of vegetarian mince
- Two tablespoons of rice wine
- One teaspoon of soy sauce
- 200 grams of tofu
- Two teaspoons of Sichuan peppercorns
- Two tablespoons of groundnut oil
- 200 grams of haricots verts, cut into 2cm pieces
- Two red chilies, or a teaspoon of chili flakes
- Two tablespoons of fried bean paste with shallots
- Two crushed garlic cloves
- A tablespoon of ginger

- 200 milliliters of vegetable stock
- A small chopped onion
- Two teaspoons of soy sauce
- A teaspoon of toasted sesame oil
- A tablespoon of corn flour
- Three tablespoons of water

Directions:

- Put the mince into a dish, add the wine and a teaspoon of the soy sauce and marinate it for half an hour
- Let the tofu simmer in salt water for 15 minutes, and then drain
- Cut the tofu into cubes
- Put the peppercorns in a dry frying pan and toast them for 2 to 3 minutes, before removing them and crushing
- Heat the wok and add in a tablespoon of groundnut oil until smoking hot. Add in the haricots verts and fry for 3 to 4 minutes until charred. Remove from the heat and put the beans aside
- Put another tablespoon of the oil in the wok

- Put the chilies and bean paste into the wok and cook for another minute

- Put the ginger and garlic into the wok, cook for a further 30 seconds

- Put the mince, stock, soy sauce, sesame oil, mince, and peppercorns into the wok and stir while cooking for two minutes

- Dissolve the cornflour in the water before adding this to the wok mixture and cook for a minute until the mixture gets thick

- Stir in the tofu and the green beans into the mixture, cook for a further minute

Tip: Tofu can taste very bland, marinating it will improve the flavor greatly.

Tofu with green vegetables and noodles

Serves: four

Prep time: 15 minutes

Cook time: 10 minutes

Calories: 197

Ingredients

- 250 grams of medium egg noodles
- 125 milliliters of vegetable stock
- Two tablespoons of soy sauce
- Two teaspoons of corn flour
- A teaspoon of toasted sesame oil
- A tablespoon of vegetable oil
- Four chopped spring onions
- Four crushed garlic cloves
- A chopped and seeded red chili
- A large courgette, halved and sliced
- 250 grams of cubed tofu
- 40 grams of watercress

- Two tablespoons of coriander

Directions:

- Put the noodles into a big pan of boiling water, lightly salted

- Bring the pan to the boil then leave it to simmer four minutes, stir the noodles using a fork to separate them

- Drain the noodles but keep around 50millilitres of the water. Rinse the noodles with cold water and leave to one side

- Whisk the soy sauce, stock, sesame oil and cornflour together in a bowl until it makes a smooth sauce

- Heat up the vegetable oil in a wok on a medium heat level

- Keep some of the green parts of the spring onions to one side, then add the rest of the onions, with the chili, garlic and courgettes into the pan. Stir-fry for around 3–4 minutes until all of the mixture is soft

- Put the tofu, the reserved noodle liquid and the stock mixture into the pan. Bring it all to the boil and stir for a few minutes to allow the sauce to thicken

- Put the noodles into the mixture and stir well

- Take the pan off the heat, add the watercress, green onions and the coriander and serve

Tip: As an alternative to egg noodles, you can use buckwheat noodles.

Chinese-style long beans

Serves: 6

Prep time: 10 minutes

Cook time: 3 minutes

Calories: 59

Ingredients

- Two tablespoons of green peppercorns
- A handful of coriander
- A tablespoon of olive oil
- 450 grams of long beans
- Four chopped garlic cloves
- A dessertspoon of dark brown sugar
- A small chopped red chili
- Two tablespoons of water

Directions:

- Crush the peppercorns in a small bowl
- Stir the coriander in with the peppercorns

- Put the oil into a wok and put over a medium heat

- Add the coriander, peppercorns, chili, beans, garlic and brown sugar, into the wok and stir-fry for around a minute

- Pour the water into the wok, cover and allow to steam for two minutes.

- Serve immediately

Tip: If you can't find yard-long beans at your local Chinese shop then you can use normal green beans

Chinese cabbage

Serves: Two

Prep time:5 minutes

Cook time:20 minutes

Calories: 150

Ingredients

- A tablespoon of olive oil
- A small chopped onion
- One shredded medium Chinese cabbage
- A teaspoon of sugar
- 1 teaspoon ground ginger
- A teaspoon of ground cumin
- 100 milliliters of sake or white wine
- 100 milliliters of vegetable stock
- salt and pepper
- A tablespoon of white balsamic vinegar

- Two tablespoons of chopped parsley

Directions:

- Heat the olive oil in a pan and then cook the onions until soft

- Add the cabbage into the pan, sprinkle it with sugar and stir

- Cook the ingredients and stir over a low heat

- Put the cumin, pepper, ginger and sake into the pan and continue cooking for another minute

- Pour the stock into the pan and bring it to the boil

- Cover the mixture and simmer on low for 10 minutes

- Put the balsamic vinegar into the pan along with the seasoning and chopped parsley

Tip: use white balsamic vinegar because it doesn't discolor the food unlike darker balsamic

Sweet potato purple cakes

Serves: three

Prep time: 20 minutes

Cook:30 minutes

Calories: 429

Ingredients

- 500 grams of purple sweet potatoes
- A bowl of glutinous rice flour
- lukewarm water
- olive oil to fry with

Directions:

- Peel all of the sweet potatoes and steam them for 20 minutes until soft
- Mash all of the sweet potatoes and allow to cool slightly
- Mix the rice flour with water to create a dough
- Split the dough into small balls
- Roll the balls out flat to create thin round shapes

- Put a small amount of the mash in a round shape and then place another round on top.

- Pinch the edges together to create a cake

- Fry the cakes in the pan in olive oil until both sides are browned

Tip: you can use normal sweet potatoes for this dish

Noodle-style pancakes with asparagus

Serves: four

Prep time: 15 minutes

Cook time: 30 minutes

Calories: 513

Ingredients

- 450 grams of Chinese wheat noodles
- 250 grams of asparagus
- Two tablespoons of rapeseed oil
- Two crushed cloves of garlic
- A small piece of ginger
- 225 milliliters of water
- A tablespoon of corn flour
- Two tablespoons of rice wine or sherry
- Two tablespoons soy sauce
- A tablespoon of fermented black beans
- 225 grams of spinach
- A dessertspoon of toasted sesame oil

- salt and pepper

Directions:

- Take a large pot and fill with water. Boil the noodles until they are al dente.

- Drain the noodles, rinse with cold water until cooled down

- Remove the tough ends of the asparagus and cut the rest into 5cm lengths

- Take a large frying pan and heat a tablespoon of the oil over a medium flame

- Put the ginger and garlic into the pan and cook for a minute

- Put the asparagus and half of the water into the pan and simmer it for another couple of minutes

- Add the corn flour, water and the rice wine into a small bowl and mix together

- Add the corn flour mix, the black beans and the soy sauce in with the vegetables

- Allow the sauce to boil before adding in the spinach and stirring

- Take the pan off the heat

- Take the rest of the rapeseed oil and heat in frying pan

- Split the pasta into four heaps and put the heaps into the frying pan

- Flatten the heaps to brown the surface. Reduce the heat and fry the heaps for five more minutes. Fry until they have a golden brown crust

- Turn the pasta cakes over and fry on the other side

- As the cakes cook, reheat the veggies and the sauce

- Put the sesame oil and the salt and pepper in with the vegetable

- Serve the noodle pancakes on flat plates and then spoon the sauce and vegetables over them

Tip: Fermented black beans are small soybeans preserved in salt so should be rinsed before use.

Conclusion

With a few simple cooking techniques, basic ingredients and the recipes from this book, there is nothing to stop you from bringing all of your favorite Chinese takeaway menu options into your own kitchen – as your own creations.

With amazing soups and starters, through to sizzling meat dishes and healthy vegetarian options, there is something for everyone in these pages.

The stir fries provide endless opportunities for varieties in flavors, textures, colors and smells, including both meat and vegetarian options.

While noodle and rice dishes provide the basis of most Chinese cookery, there are a few notably unusual dishes included, such as the fish dishes. While most of us are familiar with sweet and sour chicken, we are unlikely to have ordered any of the Chinese-style fish dishes from our local takeaway. But why not try creating them at home instead?

Part 2

Introduction

I will introduce you to best, quick, simple and easy Chinese Recipes. I have selected these recipes by utilizing a lot of time to give you best and fine recipes. In this book I have included 55 Chinese Recipes which will absolutely amaze you. This book contains all variety of Chinese recipes from appetizers to desserts.

Appetizers Recipes

Garlic Snow Peas

What ingredients you will need:

3 minced garlic cloves

salt & pepper

1 -2 tablespoon sesame oil

2 cups fresh snow peas

Directions:

1) Heat up the wok over medium high heat on the stove.

2) Put some oil in that and ensure that it is very hot, add the peas in it.

3) Fry it for a minute approximately then stir it and add the seasoning and garlic in it.

4) Quick fry it until bright green and crispy. Do not try to overcook it or it will become dull green in color and will go limp.

5) Remove from the heat and serve hot.

6) Enjoy Garlic Snow Peas!!

7) This original recipe will give you 4 servings in total.

Nutritional facts per serving:

Serving size: 37g
Calories: 47kcal
Carbohydrates: 4g
Protein: 1g
Fat: 4g
Fiber: 1g

Sweet and Sour Sauce

What ingredients you will need:

Part 1

1/8 teaspoon msg

1/8 teaspoon white pepper

1/8 teaspoon Tabasco sauce

1/3 cup white vinegar

1 cup water

3/4 cup sugar

1/8 teaspoon salt

Part 2

2 tablespoons water

1/2 teaspoon Worcestershire sauce

2 tablespoons cornstarch

Part 3

1 tablespoon olive oil

3 tablespoons ketchup

1/2 teaspoon ginger paste

Directions:

1)   Take a medium size bowl and place it over the stove on a medium high heat.

2)   Add in the ingredients of part one then bring them to a boil.

3)   Take a separate bowl and mix the ingredients of part two, stir them well to mix and add to the boiling mixture over the stove.

4)   Cook it to make it thick and bubbly.

5)   Remove from the heat and then add the ingredients of part three in it.

6)   You can use it for weeks. Just place it in refrigerator after using.

7)   Serve warm and enjoy Sweet and Sour Sauce!!

8)   This recipe will give you 2 cups of sauce in total.

Nutritional facts per serving:

Serving size: 96g

Calories: 138kcal
Carbohydrates: 30g
Protein: 0.2g
Fat: 2.3g
Fiber: 0.1g

Spiced Pecans

What ingredients you will need:

1/4 cup butter

1/2 cup packed golden brown sugar

1/4 cup water

1/2 teaspoon ground cumin

1/2 teaspoon ground black pepper

4 cups pecan halves

1 teaspoon salt

2 teaspoons Chinese five spice powder

Directions:

1)   Turn on the oven and set that to a three hundred and fifty degrees Fahrenheit equivalent to hundred and seventy five degrees Centigrade.

2)   Take two baking sheets of large size and butter them up slightly.

3) Take a large skillet, turn on the stove and set that to a medium heat, place the skillet over the heat and melt a quarter cup of butter in it.

4) Add a quarter cup of water in the molten butter, spices, salt and brown sugar. Stir it well to dissolve the sugar.

5) Put in the nuts to the mixture of sugar and cook it to coat the nuts thickly with the syrup. Stir occasionally.

6) This will take about five minutes. Transfer the coated nuts to the prepared and ready baking sheets.

7) Place the baking sheets in the preset and preheated oven and bake for five to ten minutes, or just till golden browned.

8) Remove from the oven; wait for five minutes to let stand and serve hot.

9) Enjoy Spiced Pecans!!

10) Total yield of this recipe is 4 cups.

Nutritional facts per serving:

Serving size: 276g
Calories: 428kcal
Carbohydrates: 15g
Protein: 5g

Fat: 42g
Fiber: 5g

Prawn Balls

What ingredients you will need:

1 tablespoon vinegar

1/2 teaspoon salt

1 egg

500 g raw prawns, shelled and chopped

1 stalk celery, finely chopped

1 small onion, finely chopped

2 tablespoons coriander leaves chopped

1 tablespoon cornstarch

Directions:

1)   Take a mixing bowl and mix all ingredients in it. Now make small size balls from this prepared mixture.

2)   Preheat a deep fryer and fry prepared balls in it.

3)   Fry unless balls become golden brown.

4)   Serve hot and enjoy.

5)   This original recipe will give you 6 servings in total.

Nutritional facts per serving:

Serving size: 124g
Calories: 90kcal
Carbohydrates: 4g
Protein: 13g
Fat: 2g
Fiber: 0.3g

Crab Rangoon Dip

What ingredients you will need:

1/4 teaspoon garlic powder

1 teaspoon lemon juice

1/2 cup sour cream

4 green onions, chopped

2 (8 ounce) packages cream cheese

2 (6 ounce) crabmeat, drained)

3 tablespoons powdered sugar

1 1/2 teaspoons Worcestershire sauce

For wonton chips

32 wonton wrappers

vegetable oil (in a kitchen spritzer)

Directions:

1)   Take a large size bowl and add cream cheese in it. Place it in to the microwave for about 30 seconds. This will soften the cheese.

2) Add all other ingredients except wonton chips in it. Stir it well to combine and mix.

3) Take an oven safe casserole dish and pour the dip in it. Turn on the oven and set that to a three hundred and fifty degrees Fahrenheit equivalent to hundred and seventy five degrees Centigrade.

4) Place the casserole dish into the prepared and preheated oven and bake for half an hour to make the dip bubbly and hot.

5) While baking the dip; cut the wonton wrappers in halves on diagonal.

6) Slightly spray the wonton with the oil by using the kitchen spritzer.

7) Remove the casserole dish from the oven and set the oven to three hundred and seventy five degrees Fahrenheit.

8) Take a cookie sheet or a baking stone and make a single layer of wonton in it.

9) Place the cookie sheet in the preset oven and bake for three to five minutes to slightly golden the wonton. Watch that carefully as wontons easily burn out.

10) Remove the cookie sheet from the oven and place the wonton in the plate set with the paper towels.

11) Serve the fried wonton chips with the dip.

12) Enjoy Carb Rangoon Dip!!

13) The total yield of this recipe is 4 servings.

Nutritional facts per serving:

Serving size: 210g
Calories: 730kcal
Carbohydrates: 50g
Protein: 30g
Fat: 46g
Fiber: 2g

Shrimp Toast

What ingredients you will need:

1 large egg

1 tablespoon sesame seeds, toasted

oil, for frying

4 slices white bread

8 ounces cooked peeled shrimp

1 tablespoon soy sauce

2 garlic cloves, crushed

1 teaspoon sesame oil

Directions:

1)   Take the bread slices and remove the crusts from them.

2)   Take a food processor jug and add egg, sesame oil, garlic, soy sauce, and shrimp in it. Blend it make a smooth paste of it.

3)   Spread the paste formed in the previous step over the top of the bread slices uniformly.

4) Sprinkle the sesame seeds over the bread and press the seeds in to the spread.

5) Cut the bread slices diagonally to make the small triangles from them, corner to corner.

6) Turn on the stove and set that to a high heat, place the wok over it and add oil in it.

7) When oil starts smoke reduce the heat to a medium or low level.

8) Fry the toasts in it while placing the sesame sides upwards.

9) This will take about four to five minutes or just till golden browned.

10) Serve hot and enjoy Shrimp Toast!!

11) You will get 4 servings from this recipe.

Nutritional facts per serving:

Serving size: 103g
Calories: 170kcal
Carbohydrates: 14g
Protein: 17g
Fat: 5g
Fiber: 0.9g

Chinese Spicy Beef Lettuce Wraps

What ingredients you will need:

1 teaspoon cornstarch, mixed with

1 tablespoon cold water

2 heads bibb lettuce

1 lb lean ground beef

2 minced garlic cloves

1 jalapeno chile, seeded, deveined and minced

1 (8 ounce) can water chestnuts

3 tablespoons soy sauce

1 tablespoon dark sesame oil

1 teaspoon chili paste

1/2 teaspoon Chinese five spice powder

1 bunch green onion

Directions:

1) Take a large size skillet and spray that with some cooking spray. Turn on the stove and set that to a medium high heat.

2) Place the skillet over the heat and brown the ground beef in it. Add white part of green onions, five spice powder, chili paste, sesame oil, soy sauce, garlic, minced Chile, and water chestnuts in it.

3) When starts boiling; reduce the heat to make it simmer for about ten minutes. Add the cornstarch and water mixture in to the beef mixture and stir it well to mix. Keep stirring jut till turns thick.

4) Now add the green part of the green onions and cook it till thoroughly heated. Be careful. Don't overcook it as green onions will faint the bright green color by doing so.

5) Take another bowl and separate the lettuce leaves in it. Wash it and pat it dry. Take platter and arrange lettuce cups on it. Serve with the beef mixture aside.

6) You can also serve the beef mixture with sweet soy dipping sauce.

7) **Enjoy Lettuce Wraps!!**

Nutritional facts per serving:

Serving size: 261g

Calories: 270kcal
Carbohydrates: 16g
Protein: 21g
Fat: 12g
Fiber: 3g

Chinese Wontons

What ingredients you will need:

1 lb ground beef

1 (12 ounce) package wonton wrappers

water

oil (for deep frying)

3 chopped garlic cloves

1 teaspoon grated fresh ginger

1 tablespoon soy sauce

1 teaspoon sesame oil

3 carrots, finely diced

3 stalks celery, finely diced

6 green onions, finely diced

1 (12 ounce) package wonton wrappers

Directions:

1) Take a large size bowl and add vegetables, soy sauce, ginger, garlic and beef in it. Mix it well to combine.

2) Peel and separate the skins of the wonton. Take filling a heaping teaspoon right in the center of wonton.

3) Brush the water over the two borders of the wonton skin; cover the quarter inch at the edges.

4) Form a triangle by folding the skin and then seal the edges.

5) Pinch the 2 long points together from the outside.

6) Take a deep fryer and heat the oil in it at four hundred and fifty degrees Fahrenheit. Then fry four of the triangles at a time or five if you can.

7) Place the fried triangles over the paper towels and serve them with the sauce.

8) Enjoy Chinese Wontons!!

9) This original recipe will give you 10 servings in total.

Nutritional facts per serving:

Serving size: 132g
Calories: 240kcal
Carbohydrates: 11g
Protein: 21g
Fat: 14g
Fiber: 5g

Chinese Tea Leaf Eggs

What ingredients you will need:

2 pods star anise

1 (2 inch) piece cinnamon stick

1 tablespoon tangerine zest

3 cups water

1 tablespoon soy sauce

1 tablespoon black soy sauce

1/4 teaspoon salt

2 tablespoons black tea leaves

8 eggs

1 teaspoon salt

Directions:

1)   Take a saucepan of a large size and combine one tablespoon of salt and eggs in it. Stir it well to mix.

2)   Place the saucepan over the high heat and bring it to a boil then reduce the heat to low level to make it simmer for about twenty to twenty five minutes.

3) Remove it from the heat and wait for five minutes to let it cool then drain.

4) Now add the eggs tap them over it and do not remove shells just break and crack the shells with the help of a spoon.

5) Take a sauce pan of a large size and add three cups of water, tangerine zest, cinnamon sticks, star anise, tea leaves, salt, black soy sauce, and soy sauce in it.

6) Mix it well to combine.

7) Place it over the heat and bring it to a boil then reduce the heat to a low level to make it simmer for three hours approximately.

8) Remove from the heat and wait for five minutes to let stand and then add the eggs in it. Now allow it to simmer for eight to ten hours.

9) Serve and enjoy Tea Leaf Eggs!!

10) This original recipe will give you 8 servings in total.

Nutritional facts per serving:

Serving size: 50g
Calories: 80kcal
Carbohydrates: 2g

Protein: 7g
Fat: 5g
Fiber: 0.5g

Spiced Grapes

What ingredients you will need:

1/2 teaspoon Chinese five-spice powder

1 pound seedless grapes

1/2 cup white sugar

1/2 cup water

Directions:

1) Take a saucepan of large size and combine water and sugar in it. Turn on the stove and set that to a medium heat.

2) Place the saucepan over the heat and let the water simmer just till sugar is dissolved. This will take two to three minutes approximately.

3) Remove the saucepan from the stove and add Chinese five spice powder in this mixture of sugar and water.

4) Stir it well to mix. Pierce all the way through each and every grape by using a fork.

5) Take a re-sealable bag and add the grapes and sugar water mixture in it.

6) Seal the bag and place that in to the fridge for about twenty to twenty five hours. Turn over the bag occasionally.

7) This is how grapes will be marinated.

8) Serve with whatever you want and Enjoy Spiced Grapes!!

9) This original recipe will give you 12 servings in total.

Nutritional facts per serving:

Serving size: 50g
Calories: 70kcal
Carbohydrates: 15g
Protein: 0.3g
Fat: 0.2g
Fiber: 0.4g

Main dishes

Chinese Spareribs

What ingredients you will need:

1/4 cup dry sherry

1 clove garlic, crushed

1/4 teaspoon ground ginger

4 pounds beef spareribs

1/2 cup Kikkoman Soy Sauce

1/3 cup honey

Directions:

1) Take a baking pan and line it up with a foil. Cut the ribs in to the serving sized pieces. Place the ribs pieces in the prepared baking sheet such a way that meaty side of the ribs pieces is downward.

2) Add the rest of the ingredients and brush the ribs with the sauce thoroughly. Turn on the oven and set that top a three hundred and fifty degrees Fahrenheit equivalent to hundred and seventy five degrees Centigrade.

3) Cover the baking sheet and place that in to the prepared and preheated oven and bake for sixty to seventy minutes.

4) Turn over the ribs and then pour the rest of the sauce over it or by using a brush coat the other side of ribs with sauce.

5) Uncover the baking sheet and bake for thirty minutes approx. Brush with the sauce occasionally.

6) Remove from heat serve hot and enjoy Chinese Spareribs!!

7) This original recipe will give you 4 servings in total.

Nutritional facts per serving:

Serving size: 350g
Calories: 970kcal
Carbohydrates: 25g
Protein: 62g
Fat: 60g
Fiber: 0.1g

Spicy Chinese Barbeque Riblets

What ingredients you will need:

2 pounds baby back ribs, cut into 1-inch riblets

1/2 cup tomato paste

1/4 cup chopped garlic

2 tablespoons hot pepper sauce

1/2 cup soy sauce

1 cup white sugar

1 cup hoisin sauce

Directions:

1)   Turn on the oven and set that to a three hundred and fifty degrees Fahrenheit equivalent to hundred and seventy five degrees Centigrade.

2)   Take a large size bowl and add hot sauce, garlic, tomatoes paste, sugar, soy sauce and the hoisin sauce in it.

3)   Stir it well to mix and combine.

4) Take a large roasting pan and place the Riblets in it. Place the roasting pan in to the prepared and preset oven and bake for forty five minutes.

5) Remove from the oven and pour the sauce over the Riblets.

6) Toss the pan to coat the Riblets and place the pan again in to the oven.

7) Bake until ribs are tendered and the sauce has turned thick. This will take about forty five minutes.

8) Remove from the oven and wait for ten minutes to let stand and set.

9) Serve hot and Enjoy Chinese Barbeque Riblets!!

10) This original recipe will give you 4 servings in total.

Nutritional facts per serving:

Serving size: 350g
Calories: 770kcal
Carbohydrates: 90g
Protein: 30g
Fat: 31g
Fiber: 3.6g

Chinese Mabo Tofu

What ingredients you will need:

2 tablespoons hot bean sauce

1 teaspoon white sugar

3 green onions, chopped

1 teaspoon sesame oil

1/2 pound ground meat

1 tablespoon vegetable oil

1 tablespoon minced garlic

1 tablespoon minced fresh ginger root

1 (16 ounce) package firm tofu, cut into 1 inch pieces

5 tablespoons soy sauce

1 teaspoon cornstarch

1 tablespoon cold water

Directions:

1) Take a small bowl and mix the water with the cornstarch in it. Stir it well to mix and place it at a side for the time being.

2) Take a medium size skillet and place it over the medium high heat over the stove and brown the ground beef in it.

3) Discard and drain the extra fat. This will take approximately five minutes.

4) Take a large size skillet and place it over the stove set at medium high heat. Heat the vegetables oil in it and cook the ginger roots and garlic in it for about a minute.

5) Add the tofu in it and cook again for two to three minutes. Season it with sugar, hot bean sauce, and soy sauce. Stir it well to mix and combine.

6) Now add the green onions and cooked beef in it. And then sprinkle the water and cornstarch mixture and cook for about couple of minutes or until thickened.

7) Add the sesame oil in to the mabo tofu that is thickened. Stir it well to mix.

8) Serve hot and enjoy Chinese Mabo Tofu!!

9) This original recipe will give you 4 servings in total.

Nutritional facts per serving:

Serving size: 150g
Calories: 270kcal
Carbohydrates: 9g
Protein: 23g
Fat: 17g
Fiber: 1.5g

Chinese Steamed Fish

What ingredients you will need:

1 tomato, quartered

1/2 fresh red chile pepper, seeded and chopped

2 sprigs cilantro, finely chopped

1/2 teaspoon ground black pepper

1 tablespoon grated fresh ginger

1 tablespoon soy sauce

2 teaspoons sesame oil

2 shiitake mushrooms, thinly sliced

1 pound red snapper fillets

1/2 teaspoon salt

Directions:

1) Take a basket large enough to lay the snapper flat in it. Fit with a steamer and add one and a half inch of water in it. Bring the water to a boil.

2) Season the snapper with pepper and salt and place the seasoned snapper in the bottom of the steamer basket.

3) Top the fish with the sesame oil, soy sauce and ginger.

4) Add red Chile pepper, tomatoes, and shiitake mushrooms in the basket of the steamer. Steam the snapper for about fifteen to twenty minutes or just till easily flaked by the fork.

5) Remove from the steamer basket and sprinkle with the cilantro.

6) Serve hot and Enjoy Chinese Steamed Fish!!

7) This original recipe will give you 2 servings in total.

Nutritional facts per serving:

Serving size: 150g
Calories: 300kcal
Carbohydrates: 6g
Protein: 49g
Fat: 8g
Fiber: 1.4g

Chinese Pearl Meatballs

What ingredients you will need:

1/2 teaspoon salt

1 dash ground black pepper

2 leaves Chinese cabbage

1 small onion, chopped

1/2 teaspoon grated fresh ginger

1/2 teaspoon minced garlic

1 tablespoon cornstarch

1 tablespoon soy sauce

1/2 cup uncooked glutinous (sticky) white rice, rinsed

2/3 pound ground meat

2 tablespoons water

Directions:

1) Take a medium size bowl and add rice in it. Soak with enough water to cover the rice. Let the rice soak for about couple of hours.

2)   Drain and pour the soaked rice over a platter. Take a large size bowl separately and add ground beef, salt, pepper, garlic, ginger, onion, soy sauce, cornstarch and water in it.

3)   Stir it well to mix evenly. Divide the mixture to make roll balls of one to two inches in size.

4)   Roll the meatballs into the glutinous soaked rice in order to coat the balls completely. Take a bamboo steamer of a large size and line with cabbage leaves.

5)   Arrange the meatballs in a way that atop of the cabbage leaves. Turn on the stove and set that to a high heat.

6)   Place a large pot of water over the stove and bring the water to a boil.

7)   Place the large bamboo steamer over the boiling water in order to steam the meatballs. Steam the meatballs just till no longer pink in the center; this will take approximately thirty minutes.

8)   Remove from the steam and serve hot. Enjoy Chinese Pearl Meatballs!!

9)   This original recipe will give you 10 servings in total.

Nutritional facts per serving:

Serving size: 120g
Calories: 230kcal
Carbohydrates: 14g
Protein: 15g
Fat: 11g
Fiber: 1g

Chinese Pickled Cucumbers

What ingredients you will need:

3 tablespoons rice vinegar

3 tablespoons honey

1/2 teaspoon salt

1 large English cucumber, cut into 1/4 inch slices

Directions:

1)   Cut the cucumber into slices. Take a colander and place the cucumber slices in it. Place the colander under the sink and sprinkle salt over it slightly.

2)   Let the cucumber to drain for about half an hour.

3)   Shake the colander gently in order to remove excess liquid if there is any. Then transfer the drained cucumber in to a bowl of a large size.

4)   Add the honey and the vinegar in it; stir it well to coat every cucumber slice uniformly.

5)   Cover the bowl and place it in the fridge overnight.

6)   Remove from the fridge and toss that bowl then return to the fridge for one hour approximately.

7) Remove from the fridge and serve chilled.

8) Enjoy Chinese Pickled Cucumbers!!

9) This original recipe will give you 4 servings in total.

Nutritional facts per serving:

Serving size: 40g
Calories: 60kcal
Carbohydrates: 15g
Protein: 0.5g
Fat: 0.1g
Fiber: 0.4g

Chinese Braised Zucchini

What ingredients you will need:

1 tablespoon minced fresh ginger root

1 tablespoon soy sauce

1/4 cup water

3 cloves garlic, minced

1 tablespoon Chinese black bean sauce

2 chile peppers, seeded and chopped

4 zucchinis, cut into 1/2-inch slices

2 tablespoons sesame oil

1 small yellow onion, diced

Directions:

1)   Heat up the sesame oil inside a wok or large skillet over medium-high heat.

2)   Mix frying the onion plus garlic in the very hot oil until the onion starts to become softer, regarding two minutes.

3) Stir within the black bean spices and Chile peppers, plus continue stir frying regarding 30 seconds to coating the onions with the particular black bean sauce.

4) Mix in the zucchini, ginger, soy sauce, and drinking water.

5) Cover, reduce the temperature to medium-low, and prepare for 15 minutes till the zucchini is smooth, stirring occasionally.

6) Serve and Enjoy Chinese Braised Zucchini!!

7) This original recipe will give you 4 servings in total.

Nutritional facts per serving:

Serving size: 50g
Calories: 110kcal
Carbohydrates: 12g
Protein: 4g
Fat: 8g
Fiber: 3g

Chinese Buffet Green Beans

What ingredients you will need:

1 tablespoon white sugar

2 tablespoons oyster sauce

2 teaspoons soy sauce

1 tablespoon oil, peanut or sesame

2 cloves garlic, thinly sliced

1 pound fresh green beans, trimmed

Directions:

1)   Heat up peanut oil in the wok or large skillet over medium-high heat.

2)   Mix within the garlic, and prepare till the edges begin in order to brown, about 20 mere seconds.

3)   Add the green beans; prepare and stir until the particular green beans start to make softer, about 5 minutes.

4)   Mix in the sugar, oyster sauce, and soy spices. Continue cooking and mixing for several minutes until

the coffee beans have attained the preferred degree of tenderness.

5) Serve and Enjoy Chinese Buffet Green Beans.

6) This original recipe will give you 6 servings in total.

Nutritional facts per serving:

Serving size: 30g
Calories: 55kcal
Carbohydrates: 8g
Protein: 2g
Fat: 3g
Fiber: 2.6g

China Moon Salmon

What ingredients you will need:

1/2 cup chicken broth

4 (4 ounce) fillets salmon

salt and pepper to taste

2 cloves garlic, minced

1 tablespoon julienned fresh ginger

1 tablespoon Chinese black bean and garlic sauce

1 teaspoon red pepper flakes

1 teaspoon olive oil

1 dash sesame oil

Directions:

1) Begin heating water added in bottom of the steamer pot.

2) Heat up olive oil and sesame essential oil in a saucepan over moderate temperature. Sauté garlic and ginger just for one minute.

3)   Mix in black bean sauce and reddish pepper flakes.

4)   Cook it for five minutes.

5)   Remove from temperature, and stir in chicken broth; place it aside for the time being. Wash salmon, and pat dry out. Season each side gently with salt and pepper.

6)   Take a little shallow pan. Pour black bean blend over the salmon. Put steamer pot over the boiling water.

7)   Steam for ten to twelve minutes, or until salmon flakes out easily by using a fork.

8)   Serve and Enjoy Chinese Moon Salmon!!

9)   This original recipe will give you 4 servings in total.

Nutritional facts per serving:

Serving size: 130g
Calories: 255kcal
Carbohydrates: 3g
Protein: 23g
Fat: 14g
Fiber: 0.3g

Chinese Broccoli

What ingredients you will need:

1 tablespoon cornstarch

2 tablespoons soy sauce

1 tablespoon rice vinegar

3 tablespoons hoisin sauce

1 teaspoon minced fresh ginger root

2 cloves garlic, minced

1 bunch Gai Lan (Chinese broccoli), trimmed

2 tablespoons white sugar

1 tablespoon sesame oil

Directions:

1)   Bring a big pot of gently salted water to the boil. Put the Chinese broccoli and make uncovered until merely tender, about 4 minutes. Drain and reserve.

2)   Meanwhile, whisk the sugar, cornstarch, soy sauce, vinegar, sesame vital oil, hoisin sauce, ginger,

and garlic together added in a little saucepan over medium high temperature until thickened.

3) Toss the broccoli with the sauce and serve hot.

4) **This original recipe will give you 4 servings in total.**

Nutritional facts per serving:

Serving size: 50g
Calories: 135kcal
Carbohydrates: 21g
Protein: 3g
Fat: 4g
Fiber: 2.5g

Moo Shu Vegetables

What ingredients you will need:

1 tablespoon reduced-sodium soy sauce

1 tablespoon rice vinegar

2 tablespoons hoisin sauce

2 teaspoons minced fresh ginger

2 cloves garlic, minced

1 2 cups mung bean sprouts

1 bunch scallions, sliced, divided (12 ounce) package shredded mixed vegetables

3 teaspoons toasted sesame oil, divided

4 large eggs, lightly beaten

Directions:

1) Heat one teaspoon essential oil in a big nonstick skillet over a custom heat.

2) Add eggs; put together, stirring delicately, until set, and cook for about 2-3 minutes. Take out to a plate.

3) Wash out the pan and heat over a medium level temperature, the rest of two teaspoon oil. Put the ginger and then garlic and make it cooked, stirring, until softened and fragrant, 1 minute.

4) Put shredded vegetables, bean sprouts, fifty percent the sliced cut scallions, soy sauce and the vinegar.

5) Stir it well to combine. Cover it and cook it, stirring it once or just twice, until the vegetables are just tendered; this will take you about 3 minutes.

6) Add the set aside eggs and hoisin; heat it, uncovered, stir and break up the scrambled eggs, just till heated through, 1 to 2 minutes.

7) Stirring in the left over scallions and removing it from the heat.

8) Serve and Enjoy Moo Shu Vegetables!!

Nutritional facts per serving:

Serving size: 150g
Calories: 225kcal
Carbohydrates: 22g
Protein: 10g
Fat: 11g
Fiber: 5g

Vegetable Lo Mein

What ingredients you will need:

1 teaspoon grated fresh ginger

1/4 teaspoon cayenne pepper

1/4 teaspoon curry powder

2 cloves garlic, minced

2 cups fresh bean sprouts

1/2 cup chopped green onions

1 tablespoon cornstarch

1 cup chicken broth

1/4 cup hoisin sauce

2 tablespoons honey

1 tablespoon soy sauce

8 ounces uncooked spaghetti

1/4 cup vegetable oil

2 cups fresh sliced mushrooms

1 cup shredded carrots

1/2 cup sliced red bell peppers

1 onion, chopped

Directions:

1) Take a pot of large size and add some salt in the water Bring it to a boil.

2) Put the pasta in it and then cook it for Eight to ten minutes or just till al dente; discard and drain.

3) Heat up the oil in a large sized frying pan or a wok pan. Fry and stir mushrooms, onions, garlic, pepper and carrots.

4) Add and stir bean sprouts and green onions; cook it for a minute.

5) Combine chicken broth and cornstarch using a small size bowl and add to fry and stir.

6) Add and stir hoisin sauce, curry powder, cayenne pepper, ginger, soy sauce and honey. Cook it and stir it just till it is bubbly and a little bit thickened.

7) Put in cooked and prepared spaghetti, and gently toss it.

8) Serve just after preparation. Serve and Enjoy Vegetable lo mein!!

9) This original recipe will give you 4 servings in total.

Nutritional facts per serving:

Serving size: 250g
Calories: 455kcal
Carbohydrates: 70g
Protein: 12g
Fat: 16g
Fiber: 6g

Chinese Almond Chicken

What ingredients you will need:

10 whole water chestnuts, thinly sliced

1/4 cup peanut oil

1/3 cup chicken stock

1 1/2 cups peanut oil for frying

1 cup blanched almonds

3 pounds chicken, skin removed, meat removed from bones

1/3 cup sliced mushrooms

1/2 cup diagonally sliced bamboo shoots

1/2 cup diagonally sliced celery

1/4 cup thinly sliced onion

3 tablespoons soy sauce

3/4 teaspoon salt

1 teaspoon cornstarch

2 teaspoons sherry

Directions:

1) Combine the salt, soy sauce sherry and cornstarch using a large sized bowl.

2) Add then stir Add then stir chicken; cover it with a lid and place it into the fridge.

3) Bring to heat ONE AND A HALF cups of the peanut oil using a large sized, skillet that is deep.

4) Stir frying the almonds in the oil just till golden browned, for approximately Fifty to sixty seconds.

5) Discard and drain stir fried almonds on a tissue paper towels.

6) Discard and drain all but three tablespoon of oil from the skillet. Add then stir the bamboo shoots, mushrooms onion, celery, and water chestnuts.

7) Cook while stirring vegetables for Fifty to sixty seconds. Remove it from the skillet.

8) Heat up A QUARTER cup of oil in the skillet. Cook while stirring the chicken (marinated) in the very hot oil just till pink color is vanished right at the center, and juices run clear.

9) Add and stir cooked and prepared chicken stock, vegetables, and the mixture of the soy sauce. Bring it to a simmer

10) Stir in the stir fried almonds just before serving.

11) This original recipe will give you 4 servings in total.

Nutritional facts per serving:

Serving size: 280g
Calories: 525kcal
Carbohydrates: 7g
Protein: 35g
Fat: 38g
Fiber: 3g

Chinese Roasted Chicken

What ingredients you will need:

2 teaspoons dry sherry

1 teaspoon vegetable oil

1 large clove garlic, pressed

1 (4 pound) fresh or thawed whole roasting chicken

2 tablespoons Lite Soy Sauce

1/2 teaspoon fennel seed, crushed

1/2 teaspoon ground ginger

1/4 teaspoon sugar

1/8 teaspoon ground cloves

Directions:

1)   Discard and remove neck and giblets from the chicken.

2)   Wash and rinse the chicken under cold water; discard and drain thoroughly and then pat dry with tissue paper towels.

3) Pierce the chicken completely by using a fork. Place the chicken's breast upwards, by using a shallow, roasting pan that is lined up with a foil.

4) Mix up light sherry, soy sauce, garlic, oil, ginger, funnel, with the cloves and sugar. Use a brush with the mixture of sauce for skin and cavity completely.

5) Roast in Preset oven at three hundred and fifty degrees Fahrenheit equivalent to hundred and seventy five degrees Centigrade for Hundred and five minutes.

6) Keep in mind to Brush up the chicken often with the rest of the mixture of sauce during last Forty minutes of roasting session.

7) Take away the chicken from the oven and wait to allow it to stand for Ten minutes just before carving.

8) Serve and Enjoy Chinese Roasted Chicken!!

9) This original recipe will give you 4 servings in total.

Nutritional facts per serving:

Serving size: 340g
Calories: 590kcal
Carbohydrates: 2g
Protein: 62g

Fat: 35g
Fiber: 0.3g

Chinese Stir Fry Vegetables

What ingredients you will need:

1 cup carrots, chopped

1 cup yellow squash, chopped

sea salt to taste

1 tablespoon safflower oil

1/3 cup leeks, chopped

2 cloves garlic

1 teaspoon minced fresh ginger root

1 cup zucchini, chopped

2 cups uncooked brown rice

4 cups water

Directions:

1)   Bring the water and the brown rice to a boil in a wok over high level of heat.

2)   Reduce the heat to a medium low level, cover it with a lid , and bring it to simmer just till the rice is

completely tendered, and the liquid has been absorbed. It will take almost 40 to 45 minutes.

3) Heat up the safflower oil using a skillet over a medium level of heat.

4) Stir in the garlic, leeks, and ginger; cook it while stirring just till the leeks have become soft enough, this will take approximately Five minutes.

5) Add and stir carrots, zucchini, and yellow squash. Season it with the salt.

6) Continue stirring and cooking till the vegetables are soft enough; this will take approximately Two minutes.

7) Serve it with the brown rice.

8) This original recipe will give you 4 servings in total.

Nutritional facts per serving:

Serving size: 240g
Calories: 410kcal
Carbohydrates: 80g
Protein: 8g
Fat: 7g
Fiber: 6g

Chinese Peppered Green Beans

What ingredients you will need:

2 teaspoons brown sugar

1 small red chile pepper, seeded and chopped fine

2 tablespoons water

1 cup coarsely chopped cilantro

1 tablespoon olive oil

1 pound Chinese yardlong beans

2 tablespoons green peppercorns, drained

4 cloves garlic, finely chopped

Directions:

1)   Turn on the oven and set that to a three hundred and fifty degrees Fahrenheit equivalent to hundred and seventy five degrees Centigrade.

2)   Prepare a casserole dish with a non-stick cooking spray. Heat up the olive oil.

3)   In a wok over a medium level of heat; cook it while stirring onion in the hot oil just till turns out to be

translucent, this will take approximately Five to Seven minutes.

4) Now Add water and soup; stir it. Season it the mixture with the garlic pepper and salt.

5) Arrange to make a layer of the chicken into the bottom of the sprayed casserole pan; top it with chow-mien noodles and pimentos.

6) Now pour the mixture from the wok above the arranged layers to cover. Bake it in preset and preheated oven just tills thoroughly heated, this will take approximately TWENTY to THIRTY minutes.

7) Serve and Enjoy Chicken and Chinese Noodles Casserole!!

8) This original recipe will give you 4 servings in total.

Nutritional facts per serving:

Serving size: 40g
Calories: 70kcal
Carbohydrates: 10g
Protein: 3g
Fat: 3g
Fiber: 5g

Chinese-Style Vermicelli

What ingredients you will need:

1/2 tablespoon chili sauce

salt and pepper to taste

1 green onion, chopped

2 tablespoons vegetable oil

1 clove garlic, minced

1 tablespoon soy sauce

1 (8 ounce) package dried rice noodles

Directions:

1)   Take a large sized pot of water and bring it to boil.

2)   Add rice noodles, then cook it for about Two to Three minutes or just till al dente; avoid overcooking, otherwise it will turn mushy.

3) Discard and drain. Heat oil using a large sized skillet over a medium level of heat. Fry the garlic till completely tendered.

4) Stir in noodles, and season along with soy sauce, chili sauce, pepper and salt.

5) Sprinkle the top with the chopped green onion.

6) Serve and Enjoy!!

7) This original recipe will give you 4 servings in total.

Nutritional facts per serving:

Serving size: 140g
Calories: 270kcal
Carbohydrates: 50g
Protein: 3g
Fat: 7g
Fiber: 1.1g

Chinese Chicken Fried Rice

What ingredients you will need:

6 cups cooked white rice

2 eggs

1/3 cup soy sauce

2 tablespoons soy sauce

2 large carrots, diced

2 stalks celery, chopped

1 large red bell pepper, diced

3/4 cup fresh pea pods, halved

1/2 large green bell pepper, diced

1/2 tablespoon sesame oil

1 onion

1 1/2 pounds cooked, cubed chicken meat

Directions:

1) Heat up oil using a large sized skillet over a medium level of heat.

2)   Add the onions and fry just till soft, and then add the chicken and two table spoons soy sauce and stir fry for approximately Five to Six minutes.

3)   Stir in green bell pepper, pea pods, red bell pepper, celery and carrots and stir fry another Five minutes. Then add rice and stir it completely.

4)   At last, add and stir the scrambled eggs and ONE THIRD cup of soy sauce, heat it through and serve and enjoy hot!!

5)   This original recipe will give you 6 servings in total.

Nutritional facts per serving:

Serving size: 230g
Calories: 420kcal
Carbohydrates: 47g
Protein: 34g
Fat: 10g
Fiber: 3.1g

Easy Fried Spinach

What ingredients you will need:

2 (10 ounce) bags fresh spinach leaves

8 cloves garlic, thinly sliced

1/4 cup canola oil

1/4 cup unsalted butter

Directions:

1) Melt the butter along with canola oil using a large sized skillet over a medium level of heat just till it stops bubbling.

2) This lets the water to evaporate out from the butter. Add garlic; cook it while stirring for approximately Two minutes, till it turns to brown.

3) Add the spinach leaves then cook it for about Five minutes. Serve and Enjoy Easy Fried Spinach!!

4) This original recipe will give you 6 servings in total.

Nutritional facts per serving:

Serving size: 100g
Calories: 180kcal
Carbohydrates: 4.7g
Protein: 3g
Fat: 17g
Fiber: 2.2g

Hot and Sour Chinese Eggplant

What ingredients you will need:

1/2 teaspoon chili oil, or to taste

2 teaspoons salt

2 tablespoons vegetable oil

1 tablespoon white sugar

1 green chile pepper, chopped

2 long Chinese eggplants, cubed

1 1/2 tablespoons soy sauce

1 teaspoon cornstarch

Directions:

1) Place eggplant cubes into a large sized bowl, and sprinkle with the salt.

2) Fill it with adequate drinking water to cover, and wait to allow it to stand for approximately 30 minutes.

3) Wash and rinse well, and discard and drain on tissue paper towels. Using a small size bowl mix chili oil, cornstarch, Chile pepper, sugar and soy sauce.

4) Place it at aside for the time being.

5) Heat the vegetable oil using a large sized skillet or saucepan over medium high level of heat.

6) Fry the eggplant just till it is completely tendered and is just beginning to brown, Five to Ten minutes.

7) Pour in the sauce, and cook it while stirring just till the eggplant is evenly coated and the sauce is thick and.

8) Serve just after preparation.

9) This original recipe will give you 4 servings in total.

Nutritional facts per serving:

Serving size: 70g
Calories: 160kcal
Carbohydrates: 21g
Protein: 4g
Fat: 8g
Fiber: 10g

Chicken and Chinese Noodles Casserole

What ingredients you will need:

1 roasted chicken, bones and skin removed, meat cut into cubes

1 (8.5 ounce) package chow mein noodles

1 (4 ounce) jar pimentos

1 small onion, diced

1 (10.75 ounce) can low-fat cream of mushroom soup

1 (10.75 ounce) can water

1/4 teaspoon garlic salt, or to taste

ground black pepper to taste

cooking spray

1 tablespoon olive oil

Directions:
1) Turn on the oven and set that to a three hundred and fifty degrees Fahrenheit equivalent to hundred and seventy five degrees Centigrade.

2)   Prepare a casserole dish with a non-stick cooking spray.

3)   Heat up the olive oil in a wok over a medium heat; cook onion in the hot oil until it becomes translucent, this will take approximately Five to Seven minutes.

4)   Now Add water and soup; stir it. Season the mixture with the garlic pepper and salt. Arrange to make a layer of the chicken into the bottom of the sprayed casserole pan; top it with chow-mien noodles and pimentos.

5)   Now pour the mixture from the wok above the arranged layers to cover.

6)   Bake it in preset and preheated oven just tills thoroughly heated, this will take approximately 20 to 30 minutes.

7)   Serve and Enjoy Chicken and Chinese Noodles Casserole!!

8)   This original recipe will give you 6 servings in total.

Nutritional facts per serving:

Serving size: 170g
Calories: 390kcal

Carbohydrates: 30g
Protein: 29g
Fat: 18g
Fiber: 4g

Chinese Garlic Chicken

What ingredients you will need:

3 tablespoons dry sherry

2 tablespoons light soy sauce

1 1/3 cups chicken stock

1/2 teaspoon black pepper

2 tablespoons all-purpose flour

2 tablespoons peanut oil

15 cloves garlic, peeled

1 1/2 pounds skinless, boneless chicken breasts, cut into bite-size pieces

1 teaspoon salt

Directions:

1)   Season the chicken with the salt and black pepper.

2)   Gently toss it with flour.

3) Heat peanut oil using a saucepan or large sized skillet over high level of heat. Add chicken, and fry till the pieces are light browned.

4) Turn to a medium level of heat and add and stir whole the garlic cloves; continue stir it frying for approximately Five minutes.

5) Turn heat to low, and include the sherry, soy sauce, and the chicken stock.

6) Cover it with a lid, and bring it to a simmer for 20 minutes just till the chicken is completely tendered.

7) Remove the garlic cloves just before serving.

8) Serve and Enjoy Chinese Garlic Chicken!!

9) This original recipe will give you 4 servings in total.

Nutritional facts per serving:

Serving size: 150g
Calories: 280kcal
Carbohydrates: 8g
Protein: 35g
Fat: 11g
Fiber: 0.4g

Chinese Pepper Round Steak

What ingredients you will need:

1/4 teaspoon garlic salt

1/4 teaspoon ground black pepper

1 1/2 cups hot cooked rice

1 (10.5 ounce) can beef consomme

4 medium green bell peppers, cut into 1 inch pieces

1/4 cup soy sauce

2 tablespoons cornstarch

1 teaspoon white sugar

1/4 teaspoon ground ginger, or to taste

2 pounds beef round steak, cut into thin strips

2 tablespoons vegetable oil

1 (10.75 ounce) can condensed tomato soup

Directions:

1) Heat up oil using a skillet over medium-high level of heat, and quickly cook beef in it for almost 10 minutes.

2) Remove beef from the skillet and place it at aside for the time being.

3) Beat together the soup of tomatoes, green peppers, beef consommé, cornstarch, soy sauce, ginger, sugar, the garlic pepper and salt using a wok over a medium level of heat.

4) Bring the sauce to a simmer, stir it till it gets thick consistency, and then bring it to a simmer. Add and stir the beef, and bring it to a simmer.

5) Serve above hot cooked and prepared rice.

6) Serve and Enjoy Chinese Pepper Round Steak!!

7) This original recipe will give you 8 servings in total.

Nutritional facts per serving:

Serving size: 130g
Calories: 250kcal
Carbohydrates: 20g
Protein: 25g
Fat: 8g
Fiber: 1.4g

Ground Beef Chinese Casserole

What ingredients you will need:

2 tablespoons soy sauce

1/2 teaspoon ground black pepper

1 (5 ounce) can chow mein noodles

2/3 cup shredded Colby-Monterey Jack cheese

1/2 cup sliced almonds

1/2 cup sliced mushrooms

1 (8 ounce) can sliced water chestnuts, drained

1 cup diced celery

3/4 cup water

1 pound ground beef

1 (10.75 ounce) can condensed cream of mushroom soup

1 (10.75 ounce) can condensed cream of celery soup

Directions:

1) Turn on the oven and set to THREE HUNDRED AND FIFTY degrees Fahrenheit (HUNDRED AND SEVENTY FIVE degrees C).

2) Take a baking pan and make it greasy.

3) Heat a large sized skillet over medium high level of heat. Cook beef in the hot skillet just till crumbly and browned, Five to Seven minutes; discard and drain grease.

4) Mix black pepper, soy sauce, mushrooms, almonds, Monterey Jack cheese, water, celery, water chestnuts, celery soup, mushroom soup and beef together in the sprayed baking pan.

5) Cover it with a foil of aluminum.

6) Bake in preset and preheated oven for approximately FORTY FIVE minutes.

7) Remove the foil of aluminum and sprinkle chowmien noodles above the top of the casserole.

8) Continue baking just till the casserole browns at all sides, for approximately THIRTY minutes more.

9) **This original recipe will give you 6 servings in total.**

Nutritional facts per serving:

Serving size: 240g
Calories: 450kcal
Carbohydrates: 29g
Protein: 24g
Fat: 32g
Fiber: 4g

Chinese Curry Chicken

What ingredients you will need:

1 teaspoon minced fresh ginger

1 onion, sliced

2 potatoes - peeled, halved, and sliced

1/2 teaspoon salt

4 1/2 teaspoons light soy sauce

1 (5.6 ounce) can coconut milk

1 tablespoon canola oil

3 skinless, boneless chicken breast halves, sliced

2 teaspoons minced garlic

1 tablespoon yellow curry paste

1/2 cup chicken broth, divided

1 teaspoon white sugar

1 1/2 teaspoons curry powder

Directions:

1) Take a bowl and, mash yellow curry paste along with around two table spoons of the chicken broth to completely dissolve the paste; beat in the rest of the chicken broth, coconut milk, light soy sauce, salt, curry powder and sugar.

2) Place it at aside for the time being.

3) Heat a saucepan or large sized skillet over high level of heat for approximately about THIRTY seconds; then pour the oil in it.

4) Heat up oil for 30 seconds.

5) Stir Chicken, the garlic and ginger into the simmering oil; cook it while stirring just till the chicken has started to brown and ginger and garlic are fragrant, for approximately Two minutes.

6) Stir in the potatoes and onions, gently toss all ingredients in the simmering oil, and pour in the mixture of sauce.

7) Add the sauce bring it to a boil, reduce heat, and cover saucepan. Bring it to a simmer just till the chicken is cooked and prepared through and the potatoes are completely tendered, TWENTY to TWENTY FIVE minutes.

8) Serve and enjoy.

9) This original recipe will give you 4 servings in total.

Nutritional facts per serving:

Serving size: 130g
Calories: 235kcal
Carbohydrates: 24g
Protein: 20g
Fat: 7g
Fiber: 4g

Soup recipes

Chinese Sizzling Rice Soup

What ingredients you will need:

1/2 teaspoon salt

1 tablespoon sherry

2/3 cup uncooked white rice

2 tablespoons chopped water chestnuts

1/8 cup diced bamboo shoots

1/3 cup fresh green beans, cut into 1 inch pieces

3 ounces baby shrimp

3 ounces skinless, boneless chicken pieces cut into chunks

1 egg

4 tablespoons cornstarch

4 cups vegetable oil for frying

3 cups chicken broth

1 ounce mushrooms, chopped

Directions:

1) Combine together the cornstarch, egg, the chicken and shrimp.

2) Heat Three cups of the oil in saucepan. When it is simmering, add shrimp and the chicken mixture.

3) Cook it for A HALF OF A minute. .

4) Place over mixture in pot along with green beans, bamboo shoots, drinking water chestnuts, mushroom and the broth. Bring it to a boil.

5) Add sherry and salt. Return it to a boil.

6) Turn the heat to a lower level to bring it to a simmer. At the same time, heat the rest of oil until it becomes hot.

7) Add the rice and brown them quickly. Drain and add to the soup.

8) Serve and enjoy!!

9) **This original recipe will give you 6 servings in total.**

Nutritional facts per serving:

Serving size: 170g
Calories: 305kcal
Carbohydrates: 24g
Protein: 11g
Fat: 17g
Fiber: 0.7g

Chinese Chicken Soup

What ingredients you will need:

2 tablespoons chile paste

1 pound chopped cooked chicken breast

1 quart chicken broth

1 (3 ounce) package ramen noodles

1 cup shredded lettuce

1/2 cup chopped green onion

2 teaspoons sugar

1/4 cup soy sauce

1 cup chopped celery

2 tablespoons sesame oil

1/2 teaspoon ground turmeric

2 teaspoons chopped fresh ginger root

Directions:

1) Using a large sized pot, heat up oil over a medium level of heat. Cook Chile paste, ginger and turmeric in oil just till fragrant, One to Two minutes.

2) Add chicken, celery, soy sauce, sugar and broth. Bring it to a boil, then include the noodles and then cook it for Three minutes.

3) Add and stir lettuce and remove from the heat.

4) Serve it garnished along with green onions.

5) This original recipe will give you 8 servings in total.

Nutritional facts per serving:

Serving size: 100g
Calories: 165kcal
Carbohydrates: 6g
Protein: 17g
Fat: 9g
Fiber: 0.6g

Chinese Glass Noodle Soup

What ingredients you will need:

2 tablespoons fish sauce

1 jalapeno pepper, cut into 8 thin slices

1/4 cup chopped fresh cilantro

2 tablespoons thin strips fresh ginger root

4 2-inch pieces fresh lemongrass, minced

2 ounces uncooked bean threads (cellophane noodles)

3 (14.5 ounce) cans chicken broth

2 skinless, boneless chicken breast halves, cut into 1/2-inch strips

6 large shrimp, peeled and deveined

2 tablespoons lime juice

1 large clove garlic, minced

Directions:

1)   Soak bean threads using a large sized bowl of simmering drinking water till soft, for approximately FIFTEEN minutes.

2) Drain and cut into bite sized lengths. Divide the noodles into four separate bowls.

3) Add chicken broth, the garlic, ginger, lemon grass and bring it to a boil using a large sized wok.

4) Reduce heat to a medium low level and then cook the mixture to bring it to simmer just till the mixture is fragrant, for approximately FIFTEEN minutes.

5) Add shrimp and the chicken to the soup; bring it to a simmer till the chicken pieces are cooked and prepared through, Three to Five minutes.

6) Stir it the fish sauce and lime juice through the soup.

7) Ladle the soup above the noodles; top it with cilantro and jalapeno pepper slices.

8) Serve and Enjoy Chinese Glass Noodle Soup!!

Nutritional facts per serving:

Serving size: 100g
Calories: 175kcal
Carbohydrates: 16g
Protein: 18g
Fat: 2.2g
Fiber: 0.3g

Chinese Shrimp and Tofu Soup

What ingredients you will need:

1 (1/2 inch) piece fresh ginger root, minced

6 ounces raw small shrimp, shelled and deveined

1 quart chicken stock

8 ounces tofu, diced small

1/3 cup frozen peas, thawed

1 teaspoon salt

1/2 teaspoon black pepper

1 tablespoon cornstarch

1 tablespoon vegetable oil

2 cloves garlic, minced

Directions:
1)   Heat up the oil using a large sized wok or saucepan over high level of heat. Cook garlic and ginger just till fragrant and light browned.

2)   Add and stir the shrimp, and fry till cooked and prepared, then remove and place it at aside for the time being.

3)   Add in the chicken stock and bring it to a boil.

4)   Reduce to a medium level of heat, add the tofu and peas, season with the salt and pepper, then return to a stove bring it to a simmer.

5)   Mix the cornstarch along with a little drinking water to form a thin paste. Stir cornstarch into the soup and bring it to a simmer. Add shrimp back into the soup and then serve.

6)   This original recipe will give you 6 servings in total.

Nutritional facts per serving:

Serving size: 60g
Calories: 110kcal
Carbohydrates: 5g
Protein: 10g
Fat: 5g
Fiber: 0.6g

Chinese Corn Soup

What ingredients you will need:

1 teaspoon ground nutmeg, or to taste

1 egg, or more as desired

fresh ground pepper

1/4 cup butter

1 stalk celery, cut into bite-size pieces

1 onion, cut into bite-size pieces

1 1/2 tablespoons all-purpose flour

5 cups chicken broth

1 (14.75 ounce) can cream-style corn

Directions:

1)   Heat the chicken broth using a wok over a medium level of heat, and add whole can of corn.

2)   Allow it to boil, stirring often, and reduce the heat to bring it to simmer.

3)   Using a skillet over a medium low level heat, melt the margarine or butter and then cook celery and

onion till completely tendered, for approximately Five minutes.

4) Add flour and then cook it for approximately Two minutes to eliminate the raw taste from the flour.

5) Pour the vegetable mixture to the wok, beating in the flour to avoid the lumps, and add nutmeg.

6) Put soup to heat and bring it to simmer.

7) Beat the egg using a bowl till completely beaten.

8) Stir soup gently clockwise, and slowly pour egg in to the moving soup.

9) Stir egg lightly through the soup with a fork to produce egg strands.

10) Sprinkle black pepper to serve.

11) Serve and enjoy.

12) This original recipe will give you 5 servings in total.

Nutritional facts per serving:

Serving size: 80g
Calories: 167kcal
Carbohydrates: 20g
Protein: 4g

Fat: 11g
Fiber: 1.7g

Chinese Egg Soup

What ingredients you will need:

4 cups seasoned chicken broth

1/2 cup frozen green peas

1 egg, beaten

Directions:

1) In a large saucepan boil chicken broth and peas.

2) Now add beaten egg in it but keep stirring it.

3) Finally serve it and enjoy.

4) **Total yield of this recipe is 6 servings.**

Nutritional facts per serving:

Serving size: 80g
Calories: 160kcal
Carbohydrates: 12g
Protein: 14g
Fat: 11g
Fiber: 1g

Quick Veggie Soup

What ingredients you will need:

4 potatoes, peeled and cubed

1 (2 pound) package frozen mixed vegetables

1 onion, finely diced

4 cubes beef bouillon

2 cups water

ground black pepper to taste

1 (46 fluid ounce) can tomato juice

Directions:

1) This is one of the easiest recipe in this book. Just add all ingredients in a stockpot and boil all ingredients.

2) After boiling allow it to simmer for 30 to 40 minutes.

3) This recipe will give you 6 servings in total.

4) **Serve and enjoy.**

Nutritional facts per serving:

Serving size: 110g
Calories: 230kcal
Carbohydrates: 48g
Protein: 10g
Fat: 1g
Fiber: 9g

Dessert recipes

Chinese Restaurant Almond Cookies

What ingredients you will need:

1 cup lard

1 egg

1 teaspoon almond extract

48 almonds

2 3/4 cups sifted all-purpose flour

1 cup white sugar

1/2 teaspoon baking soda

1/2 teaspoon salt

Directions:

1) Turn on the oven and set that to a three hundred and twenty five degrees Fahrenheit equivalent to hundred and sixty five degrees Centigrade.

2) Take a bowl of a large size and add flour, salt, baking soda, and sugar in it. Sift it well then add the almond extract in it with egg. Stir it well to mix.

3) Roll the dough in to one inch balls. Take a cooking sheet and set the balls two inches apart.

4) Pour an almond on the top of each cookie and press downwards to slightly flatten.

5) Place the cooking sheet in to the preset and preheated oven for fifteen to twenty minutes or until edges of the cookies turns golden.

6) Remove from the oven and wait for five minutes to let set.

7) Serve and enjoy Chinese Restaurant Almond Cookies!!

8) This recipe will give you 48 cookies in total.

Nutritional facts per serving:

Serving size: 60g
Calories: 107kcal
Carbohydrates: 11g
Protein: 5g
Fat: 7g
Fiber: 1g

Chinese Christmas Cookies

What ingredients you will need:

1 cup chow mein noodles

1 cup dry-roasted peanuts

1 cup semisweet chocolate chips

1 cup peanut butter chips

Directions:

1) Take a double boiler and bring water to a simmer. Place peanut butter chips and chocolate to melt in the top of the double boiler.

2) Take a large size mixing bowl and mix the peanuts and chow-mien in it. Pour the chocolate and peanuts mixture over the chow-mien noodles and toss to coat.

3) Take a baking sheet and line it with some waxed paper.

4) Pour prepared mixture over the lined baking sheet by rounded tablespoon.

5) Place the baking sheet on top the fridge until set.

6) This will take approximately two to three hours.

7) Serve chilled and Enjoy Chinese Christmas Cookies!!

8) This recipe will give you 24 cookies in total.

Nutritional facts per serving:

Serving size: 70g
Calories: 136kcal
Carbohydrates: 17g
Protein: 9g
Fat: 13g
Fiber: 2g